IMAGES
of America

MISSIONS OF
LOS ANGELES

A reminder of romantic mission days, the Old Mission San Fernando de España landscape is portrayed by century-old twin palms symbolic of the southern scenery of Alta California traveled by its founder, mission president Fr. Junípero Serra. (Author's collection.)

ON THE COVER: "The Jewel of the Missions," Mission San Juan Capistrano, and the bell wall, are a remarkable part of mission history. This glass plate photograph taken in 1928 depicts California's seventh Spanish mission's stone walls and tower bells after they toppled to the ground during the violent 1812 earthquake. The original bells were recovered from the Great Stone Church, completed in 1806. Its destruction, a tragic catastrophe, left 40 mission Indians dead among its ruins. The bells fell with the collapse of the 120-foot tall tower and the church's domed roof. (Author's collection.)

IMAGES
of America

MISSIONS OF
LOS ANGELES

Robert A. Bellezza

ARCADIA
PUBLISHING

Published by Arcadia Publishing
Charleston, South Carolina

Library of Congress Control Number: 2013938536

For all general information, please contact Arcadia Publishing:
Telephone 843-853-2070
Fax 843-853-0044
E-mail sales@arcadiapublishing.com
For customer service and orders:
Toll-Free 1-888-313-2665

Visit us on the Internet at www.arcadiapublishing.com

*To my son, Tony Bellezza, and his wife, Christina,
proud parents of my two talented granddaughters.*

CONTENTS

ACKNOWLEDGMENTS

The Library of Congress Prints & Photographs Online Collection has supplied the majority of images within this volume and makes possible a review of California's founding architectural landmarks practically lost through centuries of age, deterioration, and neglect. California's mission buildings were rescued only after the majority had suffered the effects of earthquakes, irreversible weathering, and ruin to the adobe walls. The work employing the Civilian Conservation Corps and photographers from the 1933 New Deal documented the progress or decay of the many iconic structures through the Historic American Buildings Survey. Unless otherwise indicated, all images are courtesy of the Library of Congress, Historic American Buildings Survey/Historic American Engineering Record/Historic American Landscapes Survey.

By the beginning of the 20th century, there had been efforts made to preserve the earliest missions, often built and decorated entirely by California natives. My gratitude to both Jim Beardsley and Chuck Lyons, from Mission San Fernando Rey de España and Mission San Gabriel, respectively, who opened the doors to my research at the original mission sites. Several photographs within this volume are released for the first time from my collection and from the Anderson family's collection of vintage glass plates. Many up-to-date mission photographs featured in chapter five are from my visits to each area.

We are truly pleased our book's release coincides with the 300th anniversary of Fr. Junípero Serra's birth. Miguel Josep Serra (Junípero was his chosen religious name) was born on November 24, 1713, in Petra, Majorca, one of the Balearic Islands, located some 150 miles off the coast of the Spanish mainland.

INTRODUCTION

SPANISH COLONIZATION IN ALTA CALIFORNIA

The dawn of conquest by foreign land and sea expeditions into Alta California brought far-seeing Franciscan padres with Spanish explorers' insight to colonize the newly discovered land in 1769. The task of reaching natives of the north and building new mission settlements replicated previous Franciscan missionaries' practices in Baja California overseen by the mission president, Fr. Junípero Serra. The first friars founded 21 Alta California mission colonies under alliance to the Spanish crown. The first settlement and military presidio established at Mission San Diego de Alcalá spawned a system over the next 54 years of huge tracts of land with many small chapels, or mission *asistencias*, connecting the neighboring ranchos. The San Diego port delivered steady loads of settlers, supplies, skilled craftsmen, carpenters, masons, farmers, livestock, and pack mules from San Blas, Mexico. The first friars' relentless devotion to their faith captured the imagination of fellow countrymen, and their exuberant expectations gained the loyalty of neophyte mission Indians inducted into the settlements as a steady labor force. Mission Indians gathered within the sanctity of the mission grounds over generations, accepted baptisms, and lived with their families under the constant guard of soldiers. A neophyte mission Indian was subjected to the ceremonies of the culture and strict daily practices while also being influenced by outlying tribal elders resisting the invaders. Among their far-reaching goals, the Spanish friars ultimately planned to entrust the developed lands at the missions to neophyte devotees in accordance with a new and more perfected way of life. In 1821, the system of 21 mission colonies suffered under the new Mexican secularization laws, and properties were divided into private ownership and used to pay off debts and extend favors. The majority of the early adobe dwellings at the missions and neighboring ranchos have long ago disappeared into the soil.

MOUNTING FORCES OPPOSING SPAIN

Although mission Indians were aligned with the industrious friars, living in close quarters near undisciplined Spanish soldiers often forced conflicts upon the neophyte families. The soldiers often destroyed relationships built by the friars in their attempts to establish an early rapport with natives. A rebellion within Mexico against its mother county that began in 1810 brought changes of governance within Alta California by 1822. The absence of Spanish ministers residing in Alta California, along with internal revolution inside Mexico City, led to a new Republic of Mexico ready to dismantle the clergy's administration of the Alta California colonies. Mexico City rescinded its solemn bond with the Franciscan friars, ending supplies from San Blas and leaving settlers dependent on support from the mission colonies. The mission Indians, who were reliant on agricultural resources and industries, witnessed the disbanding and sale of properties and ranchos. Changes under new laws within California helped foster a lawless period of politicians eager to divide or sell the mission lands, favoring Mexican *vaqueros'* control of the expansive grazing ranges. At a period of peak prosperity in 1832, many settlements had become self-sufficient but were subjected to increasing taxes and property loss. Groups of revered Franciscan friars sent to join the Alta California mission communities from Mexico City's San Fernando College were replaced by Mexican friars and secular priests. Political power diminished the padres' abilities to manage mission properties, encouraging many to flee to their homelands. The short-lived 25-year period would conclude in 1848 with the Treaty of Guadalupe Hidalgo. During the period of disarray at the settlements, Mission San Gabriel, Arcángel, was sold to private landholders, one of the last mission properties sold by Mexico's last governor, Pio Pico.

EMERGING TOWNS
On the banks of Rio de los Tremblores, today's Santa Ana River and first site of Mission San Gabriel, Arcángel, Father Serra performed the first California wedding in 1774. Fourth in the Alta California chain, the mission was moved five miles to its present location, and the existing Moorish-influenced edifice was dedicated in 1796. Nine miles from Mission San Gabriel, Arcángel, the rising population of new settlers at El Pueblo de Los Angeles dedicated an asistencia, the original church of 1818, founded by mission friars. The explorer, Gaspar de Portolá, gave the Los Angeles River its name during his first expedition of 1769 after a Franciscan chapel in Porciúncula, Italy. The name honored Mary, and its namesake, the Church of Our Lady the Queen of the Angels, was established. La Iglesia de Nuestra Señora la Reina de los Angeles, commonly named La Placita, is called the Plaza Church. Master mason José Antonio Ramirez, who was among the builders at Mission San Carlos Borromeo in Monterey, became the builder of the Los Angeles asistencia during his stay at San Gabriel. Nearby, in Orange County, Mission San Juan Capistrano had been founded by Fr. Junípero Serra in 1776 as the seventh mission, further closing the gap between missions to the north. Mission San Fernando Rey de España, founded by Fr. Fermín Francisco de Lasuén in 1797, served friendly aboriginal Tataviam tribes in neighboring regions. The mission created thriving industries producing hides, tallow, soap, and cloth in large quantities, which were then sold to other missions or ranchos. On the well-worn paths traveled by increasing numbers coming to Los Angeles, one stopover, named Camulos Rancho, was a well-known *estancia* of Mission San Fernando Rey de España. A small home and chapel provided comfort for travelers on the way to Mission Santa Buenaventura. Old adobe buildings dating back to the 1860s were found at Rancho Tejón, at the confluence of Castaic Creek and the Santa Clara River, although the Estancia de San Francisco Xavier, built in 1804, no longer stands. In 1819, the San Bernardino de Sena Asistencia was consecrated as a sub-mission to Mission San Gabriel, Arcángel. It was moved and rebuilt in 1937 with new adobe brick buildings and clay tile roofing, and in 1960, an iconic campanile was added resembling the iconic bell tower at San Diego's Mission San Antonio de Pala.

VICTORY OF AMERICAN STATEHOOD
Alta California attracted the attention of American migrants to the West, although Mexican laws discouraged it, considering the Americans trespassers. The preemptive strike of an American uprising in Sacramento took place in 1848. The Bear Flag Revolt, consisting of US lieutenant colonel John C. Frémont and 60 men, fought a small skirmish and captured the northern commander of the Mexican military, Gen. Guadalupe Vallejo, at the Sonoma Mission San Francisco Solano, the last Spanish mission. The final battles of the Mexican-American War ultimately ceded California to the United States in 1848, and in 1850, California became the 31st state of the Union. Many presidents came to the aid of the missions, including James Buchanan in 1859 and Abraham Lincoln in 1861 and 1865, who freed mission properties and deeded back title patents to the Church. All missions have been restored in modern times after continued efforts to recreate or conserve California's landmarks of the Spanish era.

One

La Misión Vieja
Mission San Gabriel, Arcángel

Mission San Gabriel, Arcángel, the fourth in the Alta California lineage, has occupied several sites. The mission was founded by Fathers Pedro Benito Cambón and Angel Somera on September 8, 1771, accompanied by 10 soldiers. A pole stockade roofed with grass and 10 huts for neophytes were built by Fr. Fermín Francisco de Lasuén and named Misión Vieja by the local tribes within the fertile river valley about five miles from the present-day mission. Father Lasuén relocated the mission to its present site after severe flooding caused the loss of precious food crops. Fr. Junípero Serra visited San Gabriel seven times and performed California's first wedding at the original site in 1774. (Author's collection.)

The Rancho Las Tunas Adobe was the home of the first friars of Mission San Gabriel, Arcángel, in advance of the present San Gabriel location. It was used for three years by the padres after the mission was founded in 1771. Purchased in 1880 by Col. Lance Purcell, the home features aged hand-planed doors and the original rafters and floor tiles. The gardens include the oldest orange seedlings, coconut palms, olives, and cactus hedges in California.

In 1775, to avoid floods and take advantage of better soil, Father Fermín Francisco Lasuén moved the mission five miles to the north. This photograph from 1885 portrays Mission San Gabriel, Arcángel at the present site where construction began in 1791. The first permanent building was completed by 1796. (Los Angeles Public Library Photo Collection.)

Mission San Gabriel, Arcángel's bell tower windows were proportioned to match each bell's size, and the distinctive design was completed in 1828. After the earthquakes of December 1812, the original square-shaped campanile in the church's front courtyard toppled and was moved to the location of the present *espadaña*. The largest bell in the background is dated 1830 and weighs at least one ton. Below, in 1902, is a quiet scene at Mission San Gabriel, Arcángel, a center of industry near the growing city of Los Angeles. (Both, Los Angeles Public Library Photo Collection.)

A stereo card from 1909 shows Mission San Gabriel, Arcángel's iconic espadaña wall's unevenly sized bells. The majestic Moorish-style mission with its distinctive appearance had to be rebuilt entirely after the destructive earthquake of 1812. Popular lantern slides like this were made in New York by Stereo-Travel Co.

The massive stone steps on the outer wall of the mission lead to the upper inside choir balcony over the church's entry. Seen in this recently discovered photograph taken in 1937, the picturesque stone texture of the massive stairs has been the subject of many mission portraits.

An aerial view from 1924 shows the quadrangle at the church. At the center of old Mission San Gabriel, Arcángel, the cemetery is directly to the right of the mission. (Los Angeles Public Library Photo Collection.)

The present day mission was designed by Fr. Antonio Cruzado and was often referred to as the "Godmother of the Pueblo of Los Angeles." Father Cruzado gave the building its strong Moorish influences, capped buttresses with tall, narrow windows, and the most unique profile among all missions of the California chain. This photograph portrays the rectory adjacent to the church's espadaña bell wall. (Los Angeles Public Library Photo Collection.)

The undeveloped landscape supported the thriving culture of the native Tongva, members of the Shoshoneian family who settled in the Great Basin of Los Angeles. In 1769, they lived within smaller villages and numbered between 5,000 and 10,000. A piece of religious art, *Nuestra Señora de los Dolores*, suddenly stopped an uprising on the day of the mission's founding after the fathers unfurled the sacred canvas. The natives put aside their weapons and brought gifts of beads and food to the foot of the painting. The precious *Our Lady of Sorrows* painting was stolen from the church sanctuary in 1977, but was recovered and is back in the church. (Los Angeles Public Library Photo Collection.)

A traditional oven is pictured at Mission San Gabriel in 1900. A rudimentary, traditional wood-fired cooking oven was commonly used in the outdoor quadrangles of the many missions and pueblos. (Southwest Museum of the American Indian Collection.)

Over many decades following secularization laws of mission properties, the mission Indians were abandoned and displaced. Portrayed here in a photograph taken around 1887, Jancinta Serrano grinds masa flour and sells her crafts. Many native neophytes remained active at mission sites after generations of cultural assimilation. (Los Angeles Public Library Photo Collection.)

The small baptistry niche remains at Mission San Gabriel today, a part of the symbolic ritual of entering the church. Within the cove, the original hammered copper font rests on the large soapstone pedestal with ceremonial pieces nearby. (Southwest Museum of the American Indian Collection.)

Tilton's 100-mile Trolley Trip left Los Angeles to spend the mornings in Pasadena at the orange groves, then went to Long Beach, Alamitos Bay, and Naples, and included free admission to the San Gabriel Mission and other attractions. This portrait, taken in 1904, was sold inside a souvenir photo folder as a keepsake of the trip. (Author's collection.)

One of the many festivities at Mission San Gabriel, Arcángel, *The Mission Play* is a pageant portraying pioneer missionary Fr. Junípero Serra and others with colorfully costumed professional actors. Floretta Cortez poses in 1938 in Spanish attire for this memorable photograph near the largest mission bell. (Los Angeles Public Library Photo Collection.)

A 1941 Founder's Fiesta was hosted by the Claretians, founded by St. Anthony Mary Claret and the Missionary Sons of the Immaculate Heart of Mary. The Claretians have had care of Mission San Gabriel, Arcángel, since 1908. (Los Angeles Public Library Photo Collection.)

Fr. Francisco Palóu recounted in his diary, "Father Pedro Cambon and Father Angel Somera, guarded by ten soldiers, with the muleteers and beasts requisite to carry the necessaries, set out from San Diego" and dedicated Mission San Gabriel, Arcangél, on September 8, 1771.

Mission San Gabriel, pictured in 1900 at its second and present site, was entirely rebuilt after the 1812 earthquake devastated much of the structure. The mission church was continually open to its congregation during years when most of the adobes within the mission quadrangle fell into ruins. (Los Angeles Public Library Photo Collection.)

A 1930s photograph shows padres meeting outdoors at Mission San Gabriel, Arcángel, at the side entry near the hand-hewn granite steps leading to the choir loft door. (Los Angeles Public Library Photo Collection.)

Alfred Robinson, an early visitor to California, attended high Mass and heard the choir at Mission San Gabriel, Arcángel, in 1829. He recounted his experience: "six o'clock, we went to the church where the priest had already commenced the service of the Mass. The imposing ceremony, glittering ornaments, and illuminated walls. . . . I could not but admire the apparent devotion of the multitude, who seemed absorbed, heart and soul, in the scene before them. . . . Solemn music of the Mass was well selected, and the Indian voices accorded harmoniously with the flutes and violins that accompanied them. On retiring from the church, the musicians stationed themselves at a private door of the building, whence issued the reverend father, whom they escorted with music to his quarters; where they remained for a half hour, performing waltzes and marches, until some trifling present was distributed among them, when they retired to their homes." (Author's collection.)

The rectory on the left is a small adobe adjacent to the west end of the mission espadaña bell wall at the rear of the church. The c. 1885 photograph includes visitors' carriages parked in the shade of the mission grounds. (Los Angeles Public Library Photo Collection.)

Pictured around 1890, the adobe buildings were once used as schoolhouses within the grounds of Mission San Gabriel, Arcángel. (Los Angeles Public Library Photo Collection.)

This view shows the church entry in 1937. An original arched roof was built by Fr. José Maria Zalvidea and developed cracks soon after the earthquake of 1803, allowing sunlight to peer in. It was removed in 1807 and replaced with a vaulted roof and clay tiles.

Jedediah Smith, an American, arrived with a party of tattered mountain men on November 27, 1826, at Mission San Gabriel, Arcángel, despite the restrictions against foreigners. They were depleted from the hardship of crossing the Mojave Desert and were greeted by the sympathetic fathers, who comforted them with lodging for 10 days. Smith was detained in San Diego, then banned from Alta California. He stole away to the north, trapping beaver and fur pelts throughout California and traveling as far north as Oregon. (Los Angeles Public Library Photo Collection.)

The rectory at Mission San Gabriel, Arcángel, is pictured in 1939. During the early 19th century, an abundance of water at the mission led to prosperous agricultural enterprises playing a vital role from the start. (Los Angeles Public Library Photo Collection.)

Producing hides, soap, tallow, clothes, and even shoes as part of the mission's enterprise were industries run by neophytes Tongva Indians. Vats for tallow soaps with brick-lined enclosures were built inside the church quadrangle. The mission espadaña appears in the background of this photograph from 1937.

An old adobe wall surrounds the courtyard corner near the church's front entry where a square campanile once stood holding the bells of the mission. Destroyed by the earthquake of 1812, the remaining damaged stone tower walls may be still viewed today. (Author's collection.)

Mission San Gabriel, Arcángel, is pictured in 1937. The street front was removed after more recent renovations to the park plaza. The mission was built originally five miles south of the present one near the Río Hondo in today's Montebello. The site was chosen in 1775 for its access to timber and firewood near the San Gabriel River. Mission president Father Serra visited the mission seven times.

Mission San Gabriel, Arcángel's Gothic appearance, with unique narrow windows and pyramidal caps atop each buttress, adds distinct architectural features to the mission's Moorish influences, unlike all other Spanish California missions. Impressive in size overall, the present-day mission, repaired from earthquakes in 1828, is well preserved after continued service. (Author's collection.)

The cemetery known as the Campo Santo was first consecrated in 1778 and again on January 29, 1939, by Los Angeles archbishop John Cantwell. It served as the final resting place for some 6,000 neophytes. The venerable fathers of the past and many native generations led their lives in relative harmony and are interred on hallowed mission grounds. (Los Angeles Public Library Photo Collection.)

Begun in 1797 above the mission's massive foundations, walls of stone were built to the top of the windows and adobe bricks were added, reaching the roof. The mission quadrangle encompassed thriving industries guided by the friars to supply the growing Pueblo de Los Angeles nearby. (Los Angeles Public Library Photo Collection.)

Displayed within the mission's hallowed hallways open to the public are rare and unusual works of art, ironwork, tools, and hardware left by the pioneer padres and keepers at Mission San Gabriel, Arcángel, over centuries. (Los Angeles Public Library Photo Collection.)

The church of Mission San Gabriel, Arcángel, has artwork of the 14 Stations of the Cross with muted, aged colors painted by neophyte Indians lining the nave. A vintage postcard portrays the setting from the early 20th-century mission, which remains unchanged over many decades. (Author's collection.)

The side entry of Mission San Gabriel church is crowned with a niche holding a sculpture of Father Serra, founder of nine early missions in Alta California, including the first San Diego settlement of 1769. (Los Angeles Public Library Photo Collection.)

Under the direction of Father Junípero Serra, Mission San Gabriel, Arcángel, was founded on September 8, 1771, and dedicated by Padres Pedro Benito Cambon and Angel Fernandes de la Somera. The construction of a stockade protected the mission after misconduct by a Spanish solider early on. The retaliating chief was killed and his head impaled, putting the mission Indians at a distance from the Spanish soon after the mission's founding. (Author's collection.)

After 15 years spent building Mission San Gabriel, Arcángel, the completed church was blessed on February 21, 1805. The 1812 earthquake badly damaged the church, padres' quarters, and workshops, also destroying the first stone bell tower built to the right of the church entry. The iconic bell wall of today was built adjoining the old mission at the rear. (Southwest Museum of the American Indian Collection.)

The Mission Play Theatre building in San Gabriel is a gateway to a mythical pageant and drama from the Spanish era. John Steven McGroarty wrote *The Mission Play* in 1911 with a story of San Diego's founding and the conversion of the neophyte Indians with lavish stage sets. The play depicted the final days of the mission era, the plight of the Indians, and their ultimate abandonment. By 1927, interest in the production supported building a large theater, which remains today in San Gabriel. (Above, Los Angeles Public Library Photo Collection; below, author's collection.)

A photograph of 1885 depicts Mission San Gabriel, Arcángel, with the vestige of an old adobe home across from the entry. The settlement had many prosperous days and was restored to the Church in 1859. (Southwest Museum of the American Indian Collection.)

In the corner of the quiet garden on Santa Anita Street, at the northwest extremity of the present mission grounds, this little house with one room was, according to tradition, used by Father Serra during his visits. (Southwest Museum of the American Indian Collection.)

A lavish theater was built in 1927 by John Steven McGroarty, author of *The Mission Play*, his best-known work, written in 1911. *The Mission Play*, first staged in the shadows of the old Mission San Gabriel, depicted the founding of California's settlements and its mission culture in a colorful pageant with Spanish fandango dancers and musicians, depicting California from 1769 through 1821 during the days of Mexican secularization. (Author's collection.)

The Mission Play premiered on April 29, 1912. Father Serra is pictured with a baptized Indian child in a scene from the play. At the time, there was great public concern over the plight and conditions of California's Indians. (Author's collection.)

Opening in 1912, the mission pageant was inspired by the Passion Play and portrays the Mission San Carlos de Borromeo with other sets. The play's great popularity and increasing attendance in the late 1920s led to traffic jams as more theatergoers came to San Gabriel. (Author's collection.)

A curio shop was created during the enterprising era of the Mission Play Theatre. At the end of the 1932 season, *The Mission Play* added up an astounding 3,198 performances; however, the Great Depression and unfulfilled New York aspirations led to the production's closing act. (Author's collection.)

This image from a magic lantern slide portrays Old Mission San Gabriel, Arcángel, as it was in 1905. Construction of the present church building was completed in 1805, and the building was dedicated in 1815. (Author's collection.)

The mission's population grew to over 1,700, and Mission San Gabriel, Arcángel, became the most successful of all southern missions with over 7,800 baptisms by 1817. The mission was the spiritual and cultural center of the cattle-raising and agricultural ranchos surrounding it.

Sculptor John Gutzon Borglum and his wife are pictured painting at El Molino Viejo in 1885. A gristmill built in 1810 was used for grain harvests but suffered earthquake damage and later was abandoned near today's San Marino. (Southwest Museum of the American Indian Collection.)

Two miles from Mission San Gabriel, Arcángel, the old stone mill at El Molino Rancho was a scene of romantic beauty, built in 1810 and operating until damaged by the earthquake of 1812. (Southwest Museum of the American Indian Collection.)

Seen in a photograph from 1895, hundreds of acres of the old mission vineyards surrounded San Gabriel, and mission friars became the most renowned vintners in California. The mission's several hundred acres of vines were originally enclosed by a hedge of prickly pear, also a prized item of nourishment used by mission Indians. Noted for the oldest winery in the state, dating from 1771, Mission San Gabriel, Arcángel, used three wine presses and eight stills for making brandy. The mission vine became part of the outdoor tavern in this photograph.

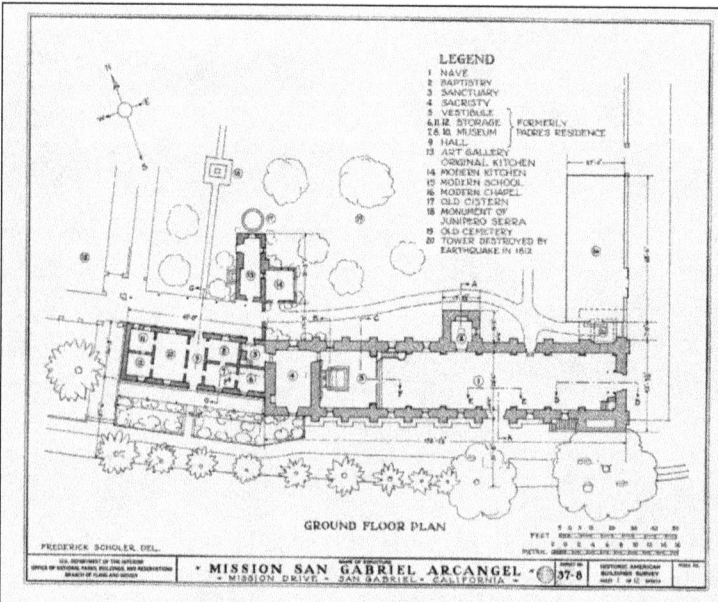

Documented during 1933, the Historic American Buildings Survey created detailed plot plans and drawings for landmark buildings undergoing preservation or complete restoration. Today, all of the 21 missions are open to the public as parks, parish churches, and main basilicas.

Two

HAVEN OF THE SWALLOWS
MISSION SAN JUAN CAPISTRANO

Mission San Juan Capistrano, "the Jewel of the Missions," was established as the seventh colony of Alta California on November 1, 1776, by Fr. Junípero Serra. A spectacular six-domed stone church was completed in 1806, designed by master mason Isidro Aguilar from Mexico. An enormous *campanario* rose high above the domes as a two-tiered spire of stone twice the height of any previous tower, visible nearly 10 miles away. A tragedy of great proportions befell the church during the earthquake of 1812, and 40 attendees were killed at the Feast of the Immaculate Conception. The bells fell from the original tower but were hung again in the adjoining espadaña the next year. The mission hosts the annual return of cliff swallows near its seaside location, a tradition observed every March 19, St. Joseph's Day. (Los Angeles Public Library Photo Collection.)

The founding of Mission San Juan Capistrano was delayed on October 30, 1775. After consecrating the grounds, Fr. Fermín Francisco de Lasuén received news of Indian turbulence and the death of San Diego's first friar, Fr. Luis Jayme. Father Lasuén departed after deciding to bury the two mission bells and raise a large wooden cross, delaying the mission's founding for one year. It was later consecrated by Father Serra on November 1, 1776. (Los Angeles Public Library Photo Collection.)

Fr. Junípero Serra founded Mission San Juan Capistrano and the Serra Chapel, actually the mission's fourth church at the second site, pictured in 1936. Father Serra first founded the mission two miles northeast of the present site near San Juan Creek in 1776 after visiting San Gabriel.

The Old Stone Church was an elaborately designed building requiring nearly nine years to complete. Its final destruction became one of the great tragedies of the era. The 1812 earthquake occurred during December's Feast of the Immaculate Conception, when the massive dome roof collapsed, killing 40 mission Indians. (Los Angeles Public Library Photo Collection.)

The statue of Father Serra at the Mission San Juan Capistrano courtyard by the bells of the Old Stone Church is depicted in this popular vintage postcard. (Author's collection.)

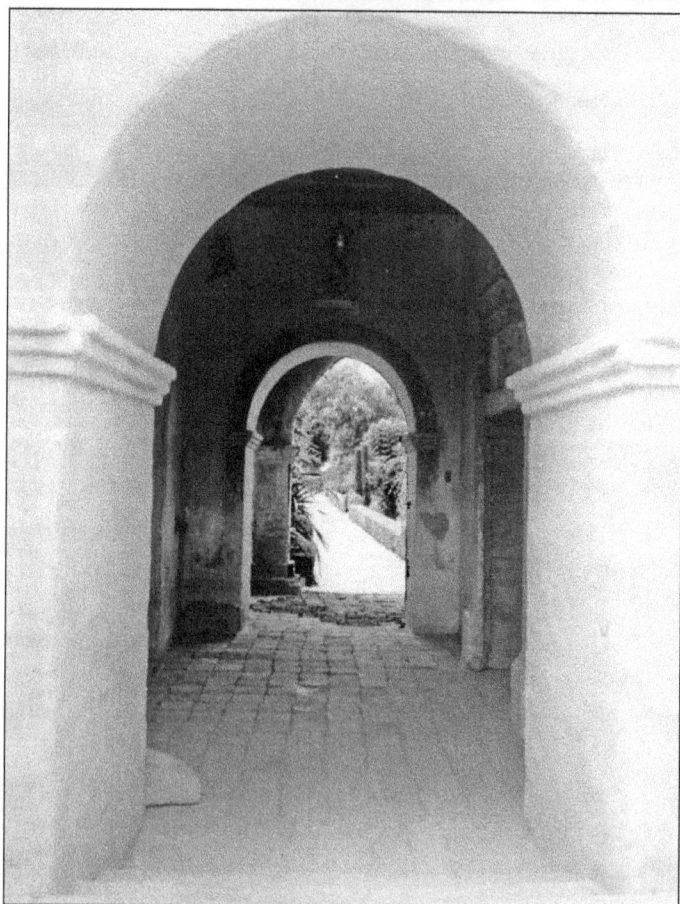

Completed in 1806, the Great Stone Church was severely damaged by the earthquake of 1812. Its tower toppled, leaving the original bells unharmed. The next year, the recovered bells were placed in the españada bell wall with a single rope attached to each clapper.

Uneven tiles line the pathway through mystical arches along smoothly finished walls and the cloistered porticos at Mission San Juan Capistrano in 1939. In 1796, Mariano Medoza, an artisan weaver, was brought to teach mission neophytes his art, yielding a period of great productivity manufacturing cloth and blankets within mission grounds. (Los Angeles Public Library Photo Collection.)

Within its northern cloister facing the interior courtyard, a small campanile sits perched above the former convent building used as a school for teaching nuns facing the interior courtyard. (Los Angeles Public Library Photo Collection.)

A flock of tamed white pigeons residing at the mission in the 1930s entertained the many visitors willing to feed them. The cliff swallows nest in the stone church ruins and traditionally return every March on St. Joseph's Day.

The Serra Chapel of 1782 was constructed entirely of adobe brick on the quadrangle's east wing. It is the fourth church built at the mission, and is where Father Serra administered Confirmation in 1783. In 1790, the roof was removed and builders raised the walls, adding more than three feet to the height of the original end of the building. By 1834, the building was completely neglected, remaining so until 1895.

The north quadrangle archways and cloisters lend unique charm to Mission San Juan Capistrano's venerable grounds and remind visitors of the initial plight of the first friars building the missions. By 1800, the mission hosted 1,046 neophytes, mission horses, 8,500 head of cattle, and a vast number of sheep. Crops totaled 6,300 bushels, and in 1797, the presidios of Santa Barbara and San Diego owed San Juan mission over $6,000 for supplies furnished.

In 1794, Fathers Vincente Fuster and Juan Norberto de Santiago began the construction of the Great Stone Church after completing two large adobe granaries with tile roofs, as well as 40 houses for neophytes. Construction was begun in 1796 and completed in 1806. The church was designed with cruciform dimensions 90 feet wide and 180 feet long and built of quarried stone with arched roof domes of the same materials. The Great Stone Church was probably the finest and grandest of all the California missions.

Visitors to Mission San Juan Capistrano in 1935 delight in the tamed pigeons at the garden. The remaining ruins in the background are from the Great Stone Church, left abandoned after the earthquake of December 1812. (Orange County Archives.)

Pictured is the west facade of the Serra Chapel, the fourth church built at Mission San Juan Capistrano. By 1922, the church was restored, and a vintage reredos and altar were added. Overall, the interior is 120 feet long by 18 feet wide, built in two phases. The building's left portion dates from Father Serra's era, before the upper wall height had been increased about 40 inches above the windows.

The ornate pulpit and upper soundboard are original to mission days. Fr. Alfred Quetu suggested Fr. St. John O'Sullivan come to visit him at Mission San Juan Capistrano. In 1910, stepping off a train, he walked a block to the corner of Verdugo Street and Camino Capistrano and saw the mission for the first time. Fr. St. John O'Sullivan was struck by the magnificent ruins and became the first resident priest since 1886.

The Serra Chapel was first constructed in 1776 and had become an adobe building in 1782. It was used by Father Serra on several occasions. The chapel was lengthened by 45 feet in 1790 and continued in use until 1896, when the roof became unsafe. During this time, Charles Fletcher Lummis, a noted historian, leased the property and continued restorations to the chapel's roof, rescuing the structure from complete ruin.

Adding an ornate reredos was part of the 1922 restoration at the Serra Chapel at Mission San Juan Capistrano. The gilded backing actually was cut to fit in place at the ends. The baroque-period *retablo* was brought from Barcelona, Spain, requiring initial conservation to its gilding. The Serra Chapel is the only original church left in the entire mission chain where Father Serra gave services.

An often-photographed portico leads to the padres' quarters at Mission San Juan Capistrano, just adjacent to the ruins of the Great Stone Church. This portrait of the archway is from a recently discovered glass plate taken around 1928. The chain of missions in Alta California lasted until 1823 and after a period of 80 years led to the establishment of California as the 31st state in 1850. (Anderson family collection.)

The abandoned Great Stone Church is pictured above right in 1919. It remains an icon of California's romantic missionary days and a legendary masterwork of all missions in Alta California. The church's Romanesque architecture and design by architect and master mason Isídro Aguilár of Culiacán, Mexico, incorporated columns of intersecting archways supporting a multi-domed stone roof. (Orange County Archives.)

Cloistered passages at the mission lead visitors on timeworn paths taken by the friars. The mission neophytes toiled to bring building materials to the mission grounds from inland creeks, carrying rocks and timber. Limestone was an essential material that was quarried, crushed, and mixed to bond the stone or bricks firmly in place to build the massive three-foot-thick walls.

The early courtyard quadrangle leads to the padre's quarters to the left of walls completed after the 1812 earthquake destroyed the Great Stone Church. It stands in ruins today, as it was abandoned in 1812 after the catastrophic earthquake toppled its bell tower, roof, and front walls.

The Great Stone Church was completed in 1806 and became the most magnificent structure of any mission, although it only lasted for six years of service. After the restoration of the Serra Chapel in 1922, conservation efforts continued into the modern century, and the building was retrofitted by 1999 for seismic safety standards. The Great Stone Church was never reused but was stabilized in 2006 to preserve it.

The immense fountain at the center of the quadrangle is gravity-fed by springs. The mission established a large quadrangle for housing, industry, and the original church, with gardens surrounding the fountain.

The elaborate Great Stone Church at Mission San Juan Capistrano rose five stories high with a roof merging six domes and a two-tiered bell tower said to be 125 feet high. During the 1812 earthquake, materials were scattered throughout the grounds. The mission's more successful years followed the tragedy, and the Serra Chapel was opened again as the main church.

The cloistered grounds at Old Mission San Juan Capistrano had been carefully restored through the 1920s by its resident, Fr. St. John O'Sullivan, and continue to serve travelers and visitors along colorful garden pathways. The large quadrangle to the rear quartered many industries run by mission Indians, who declined greatly after 1833 during an "emancipation" granted by secularization laws. (Los Angeles Public Library Photo Collection.)

The view from the Great Stone Church reveals the small coves and cracks of the stonework, ready-made homes for the cliff swallows that return to nest there each year. The remaining church dome is five stories high and still connects to ruined walls of the church.

Pictured in 1937, an enormous column supports the arched roof of stone in the mission's Great Stone Church interior. The earthquake of 1812 opened cracks in the dome over the attendees, as the sky appeared and roofing caved in. Conservation efforts were completed in 2006 to stabilize the historic ruins.

The small fountain courtyard lies between the ruined Great Stone Church and the mission's cloister of the main courtyard. The espadaña and original bells are fitting tribute and reminder of 1812's disastrous collapse, killing 40 neophyte Indians. (Los Angeles Public Library Photo Collection.)

The towering pillars and remains of the Old Stone Church can still be visited today. The church remained in ruins over two centuries after the devastating earthquake toppled its enormous two-tiered campanario, roof domes, and walls on December 8, 1812.

The ruined condition of the old colonnade and walls are pictured in this vintage postcard. The Serra Chapel at Mission San Juan Capistrano is the only standing adobe where Fr. Junípero Serra gave Mass. Fr. St. John O'Sullivan began restorations there in 1910. (Author's collection.)

All adobe construction becomes vulnerable with the loss of roofing, which increases the risk of weather damage to the walls of these simple earthen structures. This photograph, by restorer Charles Lummis, was taken after he had leased the mission and rescued it, implementing needed conservation to the buildings. (Southwest Museum of the American Indian Collection.)

Cliff swallows are found along the craggy coastline of California and are familiar residents at Mission San Juan Capistrano's ruins during their annual return. It is Mission San Juan Capistrano's best-known tradition. (Author's collection.)

A sustaining agrarian economy was created by the friars of Mission San Juan Capistrano, who also devised methods to produce larger quantities of flour using stone grinding mills pulled by animals, and in some cases, driven by water. (Southwest Museum of the American Indian Collection.)

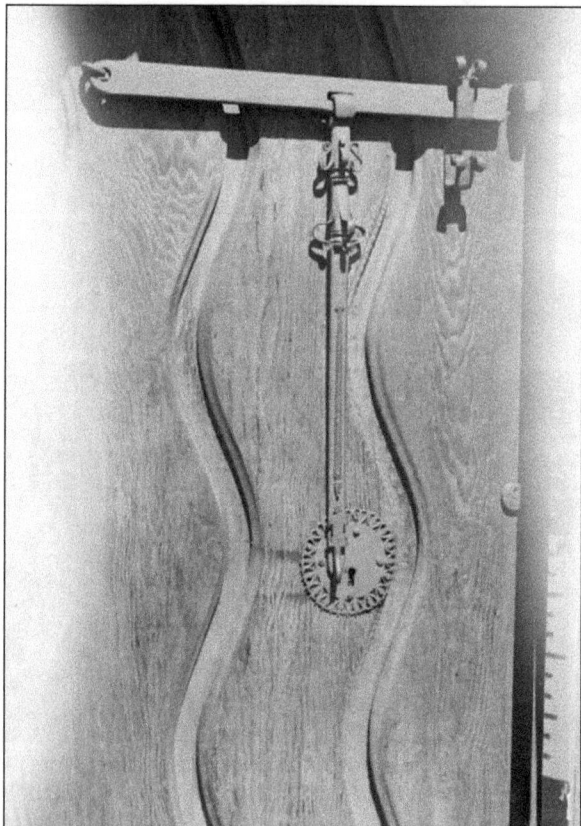

Among mission Indian carvings throughout Mission San Juan Capistrano is the "River of Life" pattern on wooden doors. Handmade instruments were commonly made by neophytes, including two used during the Easter services. A wooden board studded with handle-like irons moved rapidly from side to side with hideous-sounding noises. Another is a three-cornered box with similar irons and a loose stone that is rattled during a service called *las tinieblas*, sounding in utter darkness as an expression of the crucifixion. The church is absolutely dark, and the effect of the rattle heightens an indescribable sense of rapture among attendees.

Mission San Juan Capistrano

The name of the mission was selected by New Spain's viceroy Antonio Bucareli, who named it for Saint John Capistran, an Italian Franciscan living from 1386 to 1456. Bucareli ordered a painting honoring the mission, and it has remained there since 1776. The mission was made a parish church, a status given by the Bishop of Monterey in 1918. (Orange County Archives.)

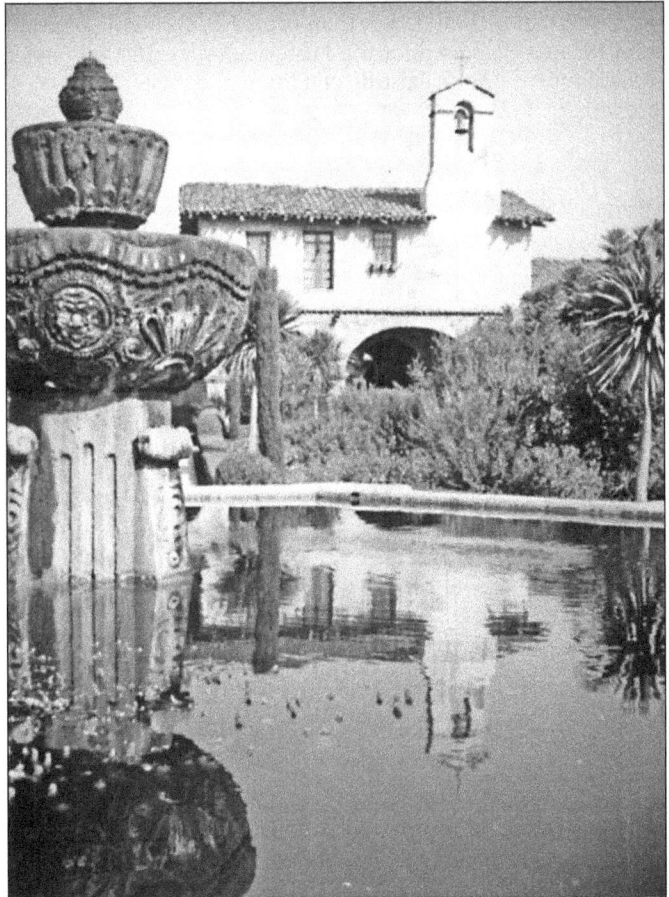

A vintage photograph within the courtyard and central fountain reflects the north end of the quadrangle cloister as it appeared in the 1930s. The mission buildings housed many industries and a nunnery in the background of the photograph. (Southwest Museum of the American Indian Collection.)

Stone facings present elaborate features using decorative cornices and a carved entablature at the entrance of the museum. Other crafted features at Mission San Juan Capistrano offer more intricate architectural design than other California missions. This photograph is from a survey from 1934 to 1937 used for the Historic American Buildings Survey, a New Deal project that recorded the mission's existing condition and measurements.

In 1937, this smoothly worn stone Indian mortar rests after years of disuse by the ancient culture of the Acejachemen. Preceding the mission buildings, the native tribe was assimilated into the new culture building the missions. (Los Angeles Public Library Photo Collection.)

A birthday fiesta in 1941 celebrates a rich cultural history at the church grounds and the heritage of Spanish settlers and vaqueros coming to Alta California. (Los Angeles Public Library Photo Collection.)

In 1938, the old Bolivian stone olive press stands in the courtyard from the days of successful industries at Mission San Juan Capistrano. The quadrangle served as the center of daily life beginning and culminating at the mission church. (Los Angeles Public Library Photo Collection.)

Precious artifacts survived years of history at Mission San Juan Capistrano, including the original documents returning the mission to the Catholic Church signed by Pres. Abraham Lincoln on March 18, 1865. Less than one month later, President Lincoln was assassinated on April 14.

A picturesque pathway leads to the guest residence at Mission San Juan Capistrano, photographed about 1937. The buildings located within remnants of cloisters have the original archways at the edges of the courtyard and surrounding garden.

The church sanctuary closely resembles the period familiar to Father Serra, the mission's founder. Thought to be over 300 years old, the Spanish reredos installed in 1923 brought an authentic luster matching the era of the first missionaries. The simple designs covering the walls in the Serra Chapel used bright primary colors made by natives from traditional sources of minerals and plants. (Los Angeles Public Library Photo Collection.)

A side altar at Mission San Juan Capistrano is shown in 1938. The simplicity of the design and its reverence have pervaded through centuries of use. (Los Angeles Public Library Photo Collection.)

In 1845, Governor Pico's stated decree considered Mission San Juan Capistrano a secular pueblo, and the church, curate's house, and courthouse should be reserved for public worship, with the rest of the property sold at auction to liquidate debts and government costs. By December, the ex-mission buildings and gardens were sold to Don Juan Forster and James McKinley for $710, the former retaining possession for many years. In 1846, the pueblo reported a population of 113. (Los Angeles Public Library Photo Collection.)

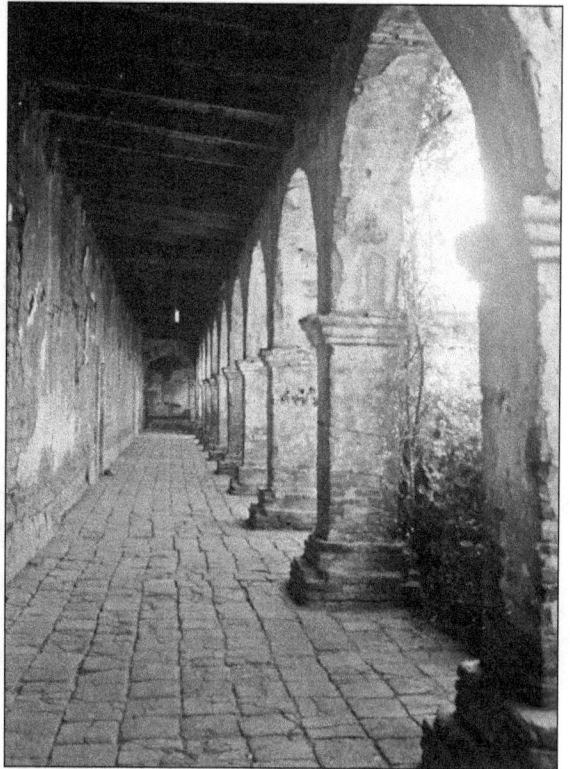

During the 1980s, construction began on a new parish church located at the corner of Camino Capistrano and Acjachema Street in San Juan Capistrano directly adjacent to the mission quadrangle. It was built on the lines of the Great Stone Church, increased in scale to be slightly larger than the original. The new church was designed by architect John Bartlett, and the interior design was researched by historian and restoration expert Norman Neuerberg, who personally painted many of the designs. The church was dedicated in 1987. (Los Angeles Public Library Photo Collection.)

The owners of an original California landmark tourist attraction, Walter and Cordelia Knott (second and third from the left) feed the pigeons with friends at Mission San Juan Capistrano around 1940. The ruins of the mission's Old Stone Church from 1806 are seen in the background. (Orange County Archives.)

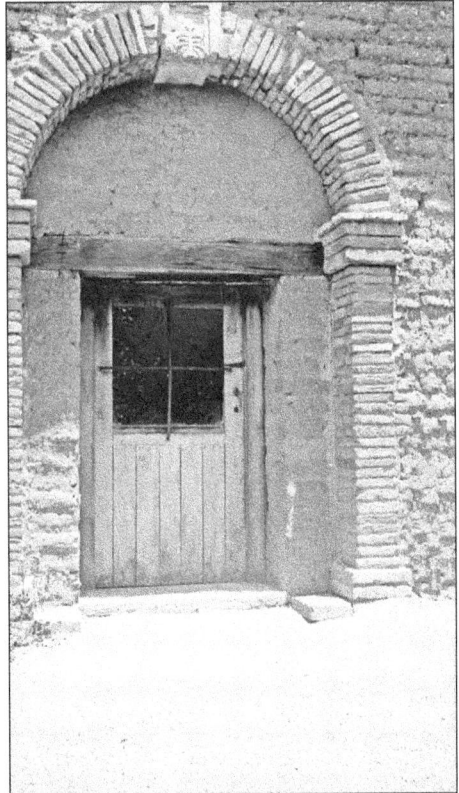

The guesthouse arch and door exhibit skilled architectural detail. Fr. Gerónimo Boscana was at Mission San Juan Capistrano from 1812 to 1822 and studied the Chinigchinich, completing in 1825 a detailed ethnographic account called *Historical Account of the Origin, Customs, and Traditions of the Indians at the Missionary Establishment of St. Juan Capistrano, Alta California*. He is the only missionary interred at the Mission San Gabriel, Arcángel's cemetery, among thousands of natives.

Mission president Fr. Estévan Tapis presided with the most elaborate ceremonies ever held at the missions to consecrate the Great Stone Church, which lasted just six years. (Los Angeles Public Library Photo Collection.)

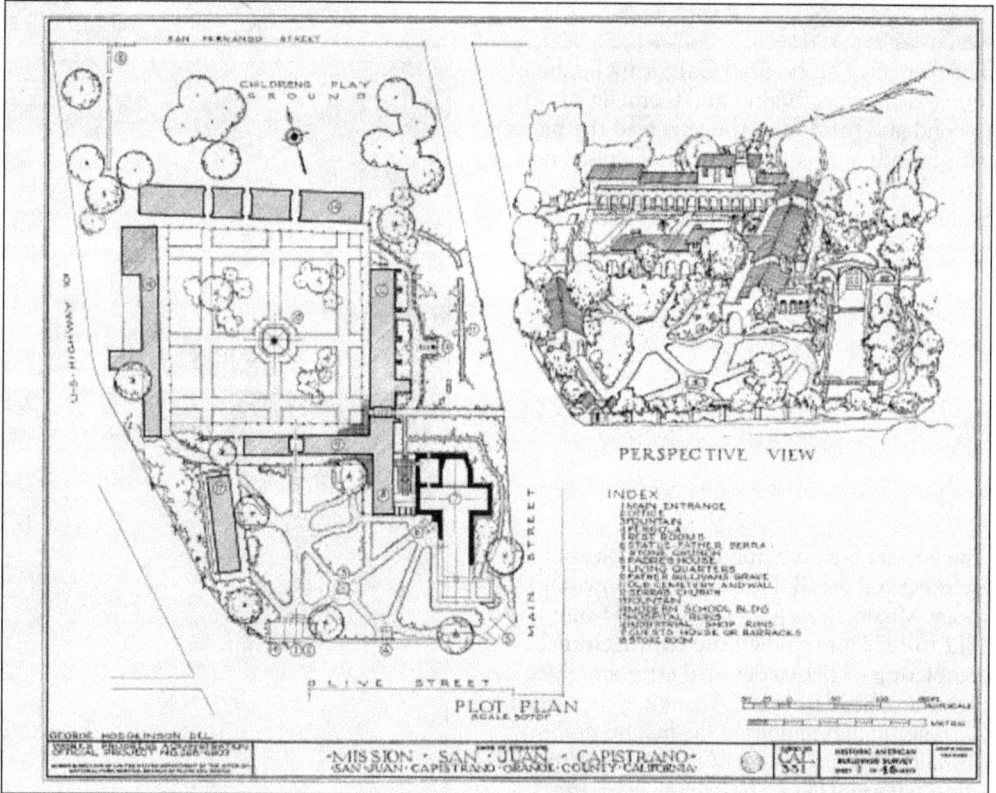

The Great Stone Church was dedicated September 7, 1806. The foundation dimensions measured an immense 180 feet long and 90 feet wide, and the roof domes reached as high as five stories.

Three

GLORY TO THE KING
SAN FERNANDO REY DE ESPAÑA

Located within the expansive barren fields of Los Encino Rancho, midway between San Gabriel and San Juan Capistrano along El Camino Real, the Mission San Fernando Rey de España was founded by Fr. Fermín Francisco de Lasuén in his 75th year. With Fr. Francisco Dumetz at his side, he consecrated the spot in honor of Saint Ferdinand III, King of Leon and Castile, on September 8, 1797. The mission was a traditional Butterfield Stage stop. The *convento*, or monastery, known as the "Long Building," remains the largest original building of California's missions, built between 1808 and 1822. By 1845, the mission came under Mexican secularization laws and was leased to Andrés Pico, brother of Gov. Pio Pico. Upon California's statehood in 1850, the mission property was divided, and the church fell into further disrepair and ruin. (Southwest Museum of the American Indian Collection.)

Mission San Fernando Rey de España became the 17th in the lineage of California's 21 Spanish missions, taking root with the help of Tataviam tribes of the area. A photograph of original adobe ruins of the church taken around 1886 records that many roof tiles fell or had been removed. (Southwest Museum of the American Indian Collection.)

The home of the majordomo was erected to oversee the property during the days of Pio Pico, the last Mexican governor of California. He headquartered his operations at Mission San Fernando Rey de España during secularization. (Southwest Museum of the American Indian Collection.)

Mission San Fernando Rey de España was established midway between Mission San Buenaventura and Mission San Gabriel, Arcángel, due to the availability of four springs, each running the full year and surrounded by rich pastureland. The convento was built with 21 Roman archways and offered accommodations to travelers in the days of the friars. (Southwest Museum of the American Indian Collection.)

A view across El Camino Real shows the mission's convento fountain. At first, a simple *enramada*, or mud-enclosed brush structure, was used by Father Lasuén to baptize the earliest neophytes. Within seven years, housing had been provided for nearly 1,000, and quarters were maintained during the following 20 years. The photograph, a recently discovered large-format image, was taken around 1928. (Author's collection.)

On June 17, 1946, members of the Historical Society of Southern California pose for a group photograph on the steps of the Mission San Fernando Rey de España on a walking tour. On the right, members hold a framed portrait. Wearing a cowboy hat at center, Roger Sterrett, president of the society, raises his hand. To the right of him are pastor John O'Connell, society secretary Ana Bégué de Packman, and architect John Austin, in charge of the society's landmarks. In the back, wearing a straw hat fifth from right, is artist Orpha Klinker. (Los Angeles Public Library Photo Collection.)

Restoration work continued through the 1930s on the belfry and the Mission San Fernando Rey de España church. After repairs from the effects of earthquakes, the church would be rededicated in 1941. (Southwest Museum of the American Indian Collection.)

At the end of the convento building, a place for a small bell exists. The distinct architectural feature of a single window stands in 1934 awaiting a mission bell after continued repairs at Mission San Fernando Rey de España were made. The mission was subjected again to earthquakes in 1971 and 1994. Each step of the way, the buildings of the church and convento have been brought to seismic standards, and the church within the quadrangle, completely rebuilt to scale, was completed in 1974.

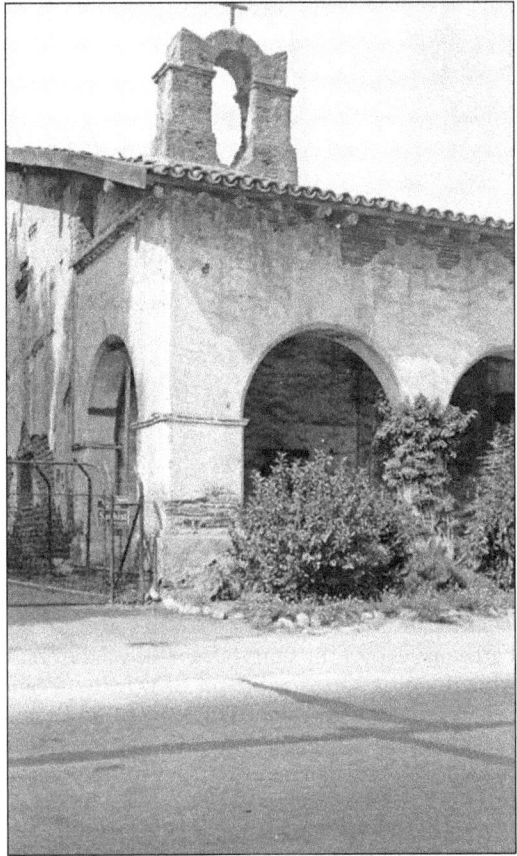

Mission San Fernando Rey de España is pictured around 1935. One can walk in the steps of the first friars throughout the complex. The convento building is separate from the mission church but was affected by the Northridge earthquake and afterwards brought to full modern seismic standards. (Author's collection.)

Earthquakes over the years have affected the church. The altar underwent generations of changes while framing King Ferdinand III within its center niche. Commonly, sacred components had been exchanged among neighboring California missions' archives, and the modern Mission San Fernando Rey de España restoration focused on authentic decorative accents close to the original. Evident changes may be seen from this postcard from after the mission church was rededicated in 1941. (Author's collection.)

This wall's three-foot-thick scalloped cornice and the door's carved "River of Life" pattern were created many years ago by native craftsmen at Mission San Fernando Rey de España. Old World Spanish craftsmen imparted their skills to talented neophyte apprentices. Designs of the mission architecture, including Moorish, Spanish, and Roman influences, were found often in printed early European texts brought by the friars. (Southwest Museum of the American Indian Collection.)

A chapel at Mission San Fernando Rey de España includes an icon of Saint Ferdinand, King of Castile and Leon in the 13th century, dominating the centerpiece. The revered king was a lay affiliate of the Franciscan Order and patron of the San Fernando College in Mexico City, where prospective friars coming to Alta California were trained. (Southwest Museum of the American Indian Collection.)

A door leading to the convento displays native crafts and decorative fresco paintings made from natural materials found in minerals from soils, barks, and tree roots. Mission Indian art was refinished and much destroyed or altered during the process of earlier restorations in the 1940s. After the 1971 Sylmar Earthquake, the church was leveled and rebuilding started. (Southwest Museum of the American Indian Collection.)

The sanctuary at Mission San Fernando Rey de España honors its revered namesake, King Ferdinand, in the center niche of a splendid golden-hued reredos featuring an 1808 poly-chromed statue above the altar. The figure was sent from Mexico City for the large adobe mission church completed in 1806. (Author's collection.)

The artistry of the Fernandeño, Tataviam, Ventureño, Chumash, Vanyumé, and Kitanemuk tribes was assimilated into mission history during the mission restorations. Original artwork was recreated with slight alterations, and significant alterations to a few designs, during restoration in 1941. Art historian Norman Neuerburg contributed restorations in 1971, returning more accurate hues to the unique neophyte paintings shortly after the Sylmar earthquake. (Southwest Museum of the American Indian Collection.)

Shaded by Mission San Fernando Rey de España's convento building portico, four residents pose for a moment in time around 1895. (Southwest Museum of the American Indian Collection.)

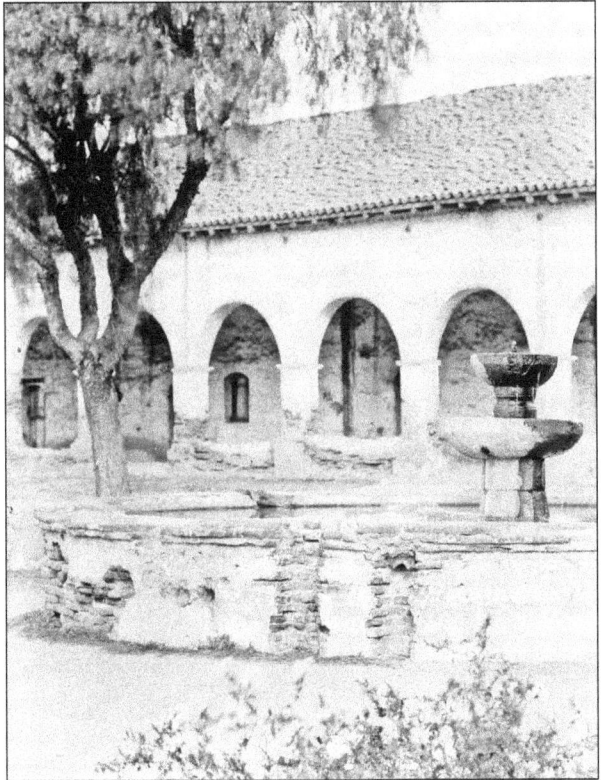

The Moorish-Spanish influences are evident in this photograph of the fountain in Mission San Fernando Rey de España's park at the convento's front. Abundant springs fed the site and served as a Butterfield Stage Line stop between Los Angeles and San Francisco. This newly discovered c. 1928 image reveals restoration keeping it in working order. (Author's collection.)

Charles F. Lummis, a popular newspaper reporter, publisher, and preservationist, became a major proponent of restoring California's early landmark missions. Mission San Fernando Rey de España is part of the Los Angeles Diocese, becoming a working church again in 1923. (Southwest Museum of the American Indian Collection.)

A view of the convento portico in 1934 shows its door leading to the fourth room. Near Mission San Fernando Rey de España, a small gold rush predating the California Gold Rush of 1849 lasted several years in the early 1840s after the discovery by Francisco López in the Santa Feliciano Canyon. Los Angeles residents flocked to the site. Later, small amounts were coined in Philadelphia by American traders. At the museum, a rich assortment of historical memorabilia includes a wine press, smoke room, refectory, and archival library housing a collection of 1,760 volumes dating from the 1500s through the 1800s.

Mission San Fernando Rey de España hosted guests traveling over the vast expanse of California's territory. The important stop at Mission San Fernando Rey de España was part of the route of the Butterfield Stagecoach Line from Fort Yuma to San Francisco for about 10 years beginning in the late 1850s.

The convento building served as the padres' quarters as well as a guesthouse offering temporary accommodations for missionaries or guests as they traveled between the missions along El Camino Real. The mission's convento building of 1822 was a large two-story adobe later used for grain storage and a warehouse for the Porter Land and Water Company. (Southwest Museum of the American Indian Collection.)

The mission fountain became a central feature at the side of El Camino Real. Located in a fertile region with gravity-fed water from four springs, the mission was a supplier of products and supplies to other missions at its peak, due to the productivity of vast livestock herds. This photograph, recently discovered by the author, is a large-format image from around 1928. (Author's collection.)

El Camino Real transitioned into a modern roadway and was clearly defined for the modern era of automobiles with bell marker signage by 1906. As in this photograph from 1934 and today, Mission San Fernando Rey de España welcomes many guests to visit the original convento museum, the largest original adobe in California.

A Moorish star rosette fountain original to the 1800s was moved as a whole to the present-day mission gardens. The fountain design from Cordoba, Spain, was reproduced in California and fed by a series of dams constructed to irrigate the vineyards south of the quadrangle via an aqueduct to the mission's grounds.

The original fountain was transported by Glendale developer L.C. Brands, who moved it to its present location within the park beside Old Mission San Fernando Rey de España's garden. Photographed by Charles F. Lummis, the massive fountainhead had been removed to relocate it.

In 1905, with restorations progressing, a church gathering could be organized again in the shade of the aged convento's portico at Mission San Fernando Rey de España. The convento was completed in 1822, withstanding many years of earthquakes and remaining the largest standing original adobe in the entire mission chain. (Southwest Museum of the American Indian Collection.)

A brick oven stands to the rudimentary building's side. Improvised designs of earlier adobes were found throughout the ranchos surrounding Mission San Fernando Rey de España. A majordomo, and at times *alcaldes* of the mission aided by Indian laborers, was given charge of large tracts of vast mission properties. (Southwest Museum of the American Indian Collection.)

Old Mission San Fernando Rey de España church, once at the center of California's pioneer days and productive Spanish mission settlements, is pictured around 1870. (Southwest Museum of the American Indian Collection.)

In this 1890 photograph, two Indian women sit on a wooden bench outside an adobe structure; they lived at Mission San Fernando Rey de España. They have been identified as mother and daughter, aged 130 years old (left) and 100 years old (right.) In 1804, nearly 1,000 Indians lived at the mission and had learned important trades, including blacksmithing, farming, ranching, carpentry, weaving, brick making, soap making, and wine making. There are over 2,000 people buried in the cemetery at the mission, and most are mission Indians. (Los Angeles Public Library Photo Collection.)

Standing neglected on the open range, Mission San Fernando Rey de España's church and quadrangle in ruins were visited by Charles F. Lummis, who found the property part of a hog farm. He roofed the old church, rescuing it from total ruin in 1895. It was rededicated on its centennial in 1897 and reopened. (Los Angeles Public Library Photo Collection.)

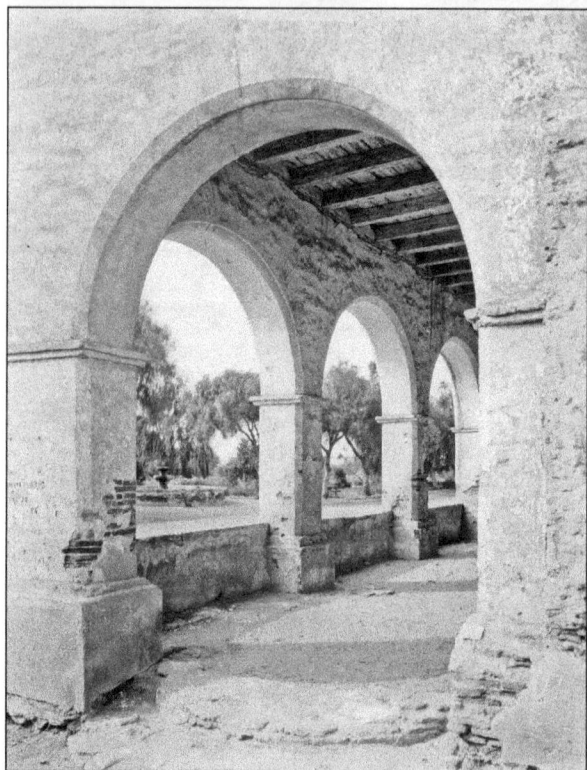

The convento building of Mission San Fernando Rey de España became a center of restoration efforts, especially at the beginning of the 20th century. Visited frequently by earthquakes from its beginning, the convento remained the only structure withstanding total ruin. It was constructed in two stories with an arcade of 21 arches. This photograph is a recently discovered large format taken around 1928. (Author's collection.)

The original adobe church at Mission San Fernando Rey de España is framed in ruins. Fr. Fermín Francisco de Lasuén began the 17th mission in California, San Fernando Rey de España, to close the gap between the large tracts of land along El Camino Real and the extant missions. (Los Angeles Public Library Photo Collection.)

This postcard view shows Mission San Fernando Rey de España's convento building after restorations were completed in the 1960s. The convento, near the Mission San Fernando Rey de España garden and fountain, features a life-size statue of Father Serra walking with a young neophyte. The sculpture is based on the real story of Juan Evangelista from Carmel, who journeyed to Mexico City on Serra's famous trip in 1773 to meet the new viceroy and plead for more settlers and a steady supply to the missions. (Author's collection.)

Evening light casts shadows through all 21 archways of the convento portico. The Mission San Fernando Rey de España church is set parallel to the convento on the opposite side of the mission's quadrangle.

Repairs have continued into the modern century at Mission San Fernando Rey de España and its convento building. The convento building remains the earliest and largest authentic adobe in California. It is a two-story building that survived a series of earthquakes since completion in 1822. This image is taken from a c. 1928 large-format photograph. (Author's collection.)

The main entry of the Mission San Fernando Rey de España's convento once faced El Camino Real's trail leading to other missions and pueblos. The "River of Life" pattern is found on most mission period doors and was hand-carved by generations of mission Indians. (Author's collection.)

The fountain is original to the mission grounds but was moved in the 1920s about 300 feet. The design of intersecting arcs is the outline of a Moorish rosette. (Los Angeles Public Library Photo Collection.)

Father Ignatius is pictured in the San Fernando Valley with unidentified mission Indians. The Tiaviam were indigenous to the mountain portals above Los Angeles near today's Castaic Junction.

Nearing catastrophic disrepair, the church of Mission San Fernando Rey de España was rescued with new roofing tiles in 1923. It stands adjoining disintegrated adobe brick quadrangle buildings restored in modern days. Charles F. Lummis began the Landmarks Club and continued restorations to many of California's earliest buildings. In 1904, he became chief librarian of the Los Angeles Public Library, and in 1907, he established the Southwest Museum of the American Indian.

A respected man of multifaceted talents and a California historian, Charles F. Lummis documented his 2,200-mile journey walking to Los Angeles for his Cincinnati paper, chronicling the changing countryside of America. In California, he became a well-known preservationist who organized the rebuilding and re-creation of early landmarks in southern California. Under his leadership, Mission San Diego de Alcalá, Mission San Juan Capistrano, and Mission San Fernando Rey de España were rescued. (Los Angeles Public Library Photo Collection.)

The convento building took 13 years to construct and was completed in 1822. The two-story building was used by Gov. Pio Pico for his headquarters from 1847 and 1861. Seen here in an early postcard view, Mission San Fernando Rey de España's convento stands today fully restored as a museum. (Author's collection.)

Approaching the turn of the century, the Mission San Fernando Rey de España church fell into ruin until, forming the Landmarks Club, Charles F. Lummis began the initial process of roofing the mission church, rescuing the building from decay. (Southwest Museum of the American Indian Collection.)

Adobe bricks mixed and poured by hand weigh about 60 pounds each. Each brick was turned as it dried in the sun. Roof tiles, first used in the northern missions, were used throughout all 21 missions to prevent attacks with flaming arrows or other misfortunes. (Southwest Museum of the American Indian Collection.)

A turn-of-the-century photograph looks west at the end of the convento building on the right and the old mission church in the center. (Southwest Museum of the American Indian Collection.)

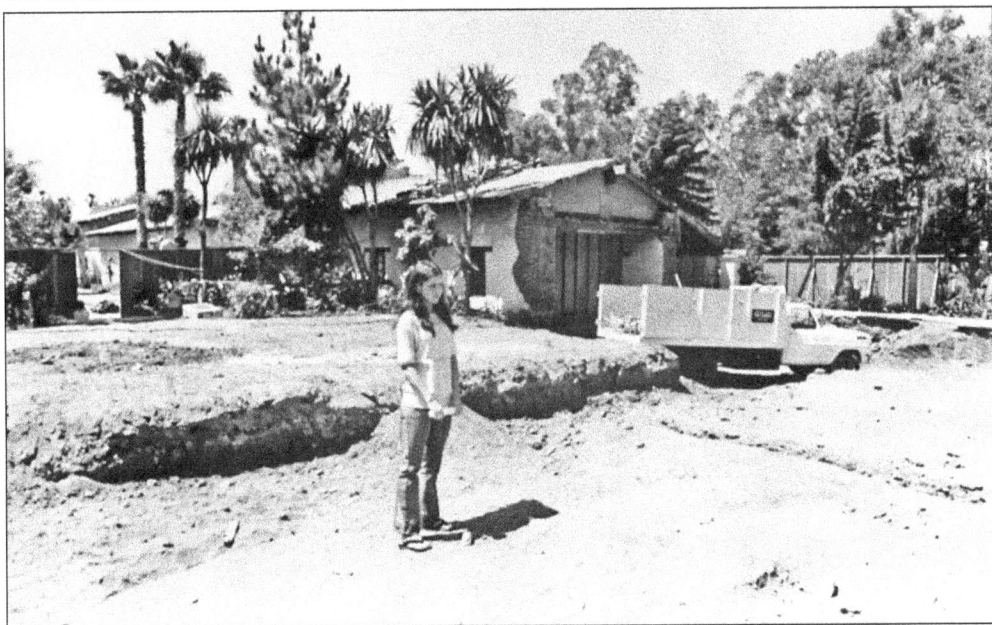

Archeology is an important key to the modern restoration process followed at many California mission sites. The Mission San Fernando Rey de España church was leveled before restoration after the 1971 Sylmar Earthquake. Kathy Gard, 15, of Mission Hills, stands at the site of the Mission San Fernando chapel. The chapel was torn down due to damage sustained from the February 1971 earthquake. (Los Angeles Public Library Photo Collection.)

Mission San Fernando Rey de España is seen as it appeared in 1938. Large piles of adobe bricks were manufactured by hand and sun-dried to repair walls and the belfry on the right side of the building. (Southwest Museum of the American Indian Collection.)

Observing the details of the old ruins reveals an epic story of age and wear over centuries of weathering and neglect. Many native designs were destroyed or covered with whitewashes and were later recreated from photographs in the new replica church rededicated in 1974. (Southwest Museum of the American Indian Collection.)

In 1896, Mission San Fernando Rey de España's church structure was a curiosity, a favorite of onlookers. A movement stirring its reconstruction was important to several preservation efforts by the turn of the century. (Southwest Museum of the American Indian Collection.)

Towards the end of the 19th century, Charles F. Lummis began the church restoration process at Mission San Fernando Rey de España, preserving the building from further weathering by covering it with a new roof. It was rededicated in 1923 but again suffered earthquake damage. In 1976, it was completely cleared and recreated to authentic dimensions using modern materials.

Cracks created by earthquakes in the mission church walls and the campanile were attended to with needed restoration through the 1930s, and the church was again rededicated in 1941. (Los Angeles Public Library Photo Collection.)

The kitchen staircase leads to the wood-fired oven at Mission San Fernando Rey de España, no longer part of existing structures and a feature attributed to the convento building. In the photograph, an adobe wall has been retrofitted for electricity in the early part of the 20th century. (Los Angeles Public Library Photo Collection.)

The convento, the monastery building facing the outer quadrangle and Old El Camino Real at the entry of Mission San Fernando Rey de España, leads to the church behind it. A young companion of Father Serra, Juan Evangelista José was a mission Indian from Carmel who traveled to Mexico City on Serra's famous journey to bolster supplies for his mission colonies. José suffered from a severe sickness but regained his health and was confirmed by the archbishop in 1773 in Mexico City. Later returning to re-educate his homeland people, and married by Father Serra, José tragically was overcome by the measles epidemic in 1776 along with his wife. (Anderson Family Collection.)

Seen through the portico's colonnade at the mission's convento building in 1937, a view of the park and fountain extends along the edge of the old mission property. L.C. Brands developed the park and moved the early 1800s Spanish Moorish fountain about 300 feet, creating Brands Park near another original fountain at the mission. (Los Angeles Public Library Photo Collection.)

This 1934 view from the church looks towards the monastery's north elevation. The scaffold was used during the period of 1930s restorations until the campanile was restored at the church's side.

Franciscan novitiates coming to church instruction included the intricate rituals associated with ringing the mission bells. They were used to mark mealtimes, to call the residents to work and religious services, for births and funerals, and to signal the approach of a ship or a returning missionary.

Attention over the decades to preserving Mission San Fernando Rey de España was dashed after the severity of the Sylmar Earthquake of 1971. A final decision was made to rebuild the mission church entirely. After years of preservation work to save the building, it became unsalvageable after the seismic force tore through its adobe walls. Fr. Eugene Frilot contemplates the quake's damage to the 165-year-old sanctuary. (Los Angeles Public Library Photo Collection.)

The church of 1806 at Mission San Fernando Rey de España had survived with continuous care after 1895. The earthquake of 1812, which toppled the Great Stone Church at Mission San Juan Capistrano, also affected the San Fernando mission's structural vulnerability for collapsing. In 1971, 13th-century statues toppled and broke but were recovered. (Los Angeles Public Library Photo Collection.)

The front adobe wall and portico of the convento building and monastery lie along El Camino Real, the vital pathway leading to San Gabriel, Los Angeles, and Mexico City. The rear wall of the building faces the mission church within the quadrangle of Mission San Fernando Rey de España. (Southwest Museum of the American Indian Collection.)

The oldest, largest original adobe building in California, the two-story convento monastery of 1814 at Mission San Fernando Rey de España is a distinctive building with 19 front archways and two arches at each end of the portico. The building dimensions are 243 feet by 50 feet.

Four

OUTLYING ASISTENCIAS
AND ESTACIONES
LA PLACITA

La Placita, the Los Angeles Plaza Church, rings its bell to signal the hour to parishioners from a scaffolding, or tripod, as in the earliest days. An asistencia of Mission San Gabriel, Arcángel, nine miles away, La Iglesia de Nuestra Señora la Reina de los Angeles was established in 1784. Gaspar de Portolá explored the area in 1769, and named it for a chapel honoring the Holy Mother in Assisi, Italy. By 1814, settlers of El Pueblo de Los Angeles were granted permission to establish a church at the plaza and the first church building was begun and later dedicated on December 8, 1822. (Los Angeles Public Library Photo Collection.)

The image above is considered the earliest Los Angeles photograph extant, taken around 1860. At the right is La Placita, or Plaza Church, and at upper right is El Aliso, a large sycamore tree that was known as a favorite place to meet. The first water reservoir is the brick building in the center of the plaza. Below is an 1889 view of the busy streets at the Los Angeles Plaza. (Both, Southwest Museum of the American Indian Collection.)

Seen in this photograph taken around 1864, La Placita was at the center of early El Pueblo de Los Angeles. The first adobe, named La Iglesia de Nuestra Señora de los Angeles, or the Church of Our Lady of the Angels, was established when Fr. Luis Gil y Taboada laid its cornerstone in 1814. El Pueblo de Los Angeles was founded in 1781 in a town quadrangle, but the first settlers' delay building the church had, by tradition, contributions from missions as far north as Mission San Miguel, with donations of cattle, brandy, and wine to be sold providing the necessary funds. The church had been rebuilt by stonecutter José Antonio Ramirez and completed in December 1822. Ramirez, living in San Gabriel, had previously constructed both the San Carlos Royal Presidio Chapel in Monterey and Mission San Carlos Borromeo de Rio del Carmelo in 1797. (Southwest Museum of the American Indian Collection.)

Fr. Joaquin Adam is pictured at the turn of the century at the parish church. La Iglesia de Nuestra Señora de los Angeles historically served Hispanic populations over many generations, as St. Vibiana Cathedral after 1876 served attendees with English-speaking pastors at the Catholic parish nearby. (Southwest Museum of the American Indian Collection.)

La Placita is pictured around 1890. It was deemed an asistencia to Mission San Gabriel, Arcángel, and was visited by Father Serra in 1783 during his last sojourn at his mission settlements. The church, built from stone, adobe, and *ladrillo* (brick), was constructed by master mason and stonecutter José Antonio Ramirez. (Southwest Museum of the American Indian Collection.)

Taken during the 1880s, this early photograph displays Los Angeles with a population of around 11,500. By 1890, after a boom, the population had increased to over 50,000. The plaza was relocated as many as four times, and the existing location was chosen for the church founded on August 18, 1814, by Franciscan Fr. Luis Gil y Taboada. (Los Angeles Public Library Photo Collection.)

This 1899 profile shows the gazebo-styled campanile from the 1860s, later remodeled to the current espadaña style. Dedicated in the 1820s, the plaza became a commercial center and site of many festivals and celebrations. The plaza displays statues dedicated to three important figures in the city's history: King Carlos III of Spain, the monarch reigning over the mission period; Felipe de Neve, the Spanish governor of the Californias who selected the site of the pueblo; and Fr. Junípero Serra, founder and first head of the Alta California missions. (Los Angeles Public Library Photo Collection.)

Los Angeles is pictured looking east in the 1930s from Fort Hill across the Plaza from the Olvera Adobe. La Iglesia de Nuestra Señora de los Angeles is in the center with padres' quarters, a school, and a courtyard planted in citrus. (Southwest Museum of the American Indian Collection.)

A view in 1880 of the Los Angeles Plaza shows the busy intersection of industry and social gatherings. The church was founded in 1814 and dedicated by 1822. The church was a sub-mission or asistencia of Mission San Gabriel, Arcángel. (Southwest Museum of the American Indian Collection.)

At the turn of the century, La Placita was known as the Church of Our Lady the Queen of the Angels. The structure had incorporated a three-bell campanario or bell wall, later removed and replaced by a gazebo-like structure in 1861. (Southwest Museum of the American Indian Collection.)

A statue honoring the Church of Our Lady the Queen of the Angels stands in the foreground, framed behind by Our Lady of Guadalupe in the painting on the walls of La Placita and all California Spanish missions. (Southwest Museum of the American Indian Collection.)

El Pueblo de Nuestra Señora la Reina de los Angeles del Río de Porciúncula was named by explorer Gaspar de Portolá in honor of the chapel of St. Francis in Assisi, Italy, honoring the Holy Mother. In the photograph, the altar is set for the Feast of Corpus Christi to commemorate the institution of the Holy Eucharist in the Church. (Los Angeles Public Library Photo Collection.)

The town was founded in 1781, and the church was completed in 1822. It added the Victorian style gazebo housing the bells by 1861. (Los Angeles Public Library Photo Collection.)

An 1880s street scene shows morning visits beginning at the church. The population of Los Angeles had grown to over 100,000 by 1900. (Los Angeles Public Library Photo Collection.)

The church was located near the river Gaspar de Portolá named El Río de Nuestra Señora La Reina de Los Ángeles de Porciúncula in 1769 in reference to the Portiuncula, an ancient church in Assisi, Italy, dedicated to Mary under the title Our Lady of the Angels. An asistencia to San Gabriel, Arcángel, La Placita was originally constructed for the early residents nine miles away from the Los Angeles pueblo. (Southwest Museum of the American Indian Collection.)

99

The 1931 photograph above, taken at the Los Angeles Plaza, shows revelers enjoying a patriotic Fourth of July ceremony. Behind the streetcar in the 1925 photograph below are the Hotel Pacific, the office of Philip Morici and Co., and Agencia Italiana, the grocery store of Giovanni Piuma, a well-known California vintner. The area north of the Plaza was at this time an Italian neighborhood. (Both, Los Angeles Public Library Photo Collection.)

Fort Moore Hill (top center), a US military installation, became a prominent landmark overlooking the Los Angeles pueblo and featured a commanding view. It was removed in 1949, and the Hollywood Freeway now runs near the site. (Los Angeles Public Library Photo Collection.)

Mission bells were important to daily life. Their harmonious peal rang to mark mealtimes and would also call the mission residents to work and religious services. (Southwest Museum of the American Indian Collection.)

La Placita is pictured prior to 1869, with fencing around the first open brick reservoir built by William Dryden and his LA Water Works Co. Father Adams had remarked, "Where Buena Vista is now open, north on the hill stood a chapel from 1784 to 1812 where a friar from San Gabriel Mission said mass every Sunday and holidays." The fence around the Plaza was built by the owner of the reservoir (at extreme right). Later, the Plaza was planted with trees and improved. (Los Angeles Public Library Photo Collection.)

The Plaza was landscaped in 1871 and served as a public park. A fountain now replaced the brick water storage tank developed in 1858 to supply the growing town. The Los Angeles River was diverted through wooden pipelines and Zanja Madre, the "Mother Ditch," to carry the water supply to an open reservoir.

This 1945 photograph shows the nave and sanctuary at la Placita, La Iglesia de Nuestra Señora la Reina de los Angeles. (Southwest Museum of the American Indian Collection.)

Many beautiful works of art held at the California missions with relics of the period often pre-date the era of the missions and were shipped or brought directly by friars coming to Alta California. (Southwest Museum of the American Indian Collection.)

According to the sign above the awning, "giant malts" and "coloso ice cream cones" were found at this Mexican store in 1937. Located at 523 North Main Street, the store was adjacent to the Plaza Church.

A photograph from 1934 shows La Placita and Main Street. As the city of Los Angeles grew, the church was surrounded by businesses. Los Angeles Plaza was dedicated as a public park in 1869. The bell wall was rebuilt to match the architecture of the original 1814 structure.

This postcard view shows the Plaza Church, La Placita. It serves multitudes inside the city today. The church had been rebuilt in 1861 using the original materials of the earlier church it replaced. (Author's collection.)

The espadaña holding the mission bells replaced the octagon gazebo of 1861. On special occasions, bell ringing marked births and funerals or a returning missionary, and at other times, novices were instructed in the intricate rituals associated with mission bells. (Southwest Museum of the American Indian Collection.)

A ceremony salutes Gaspar de Portolá's first route to explore Monterey, accompanied by Capt. Don Fernando Rivera y Moncada, Lt. Don Pedro Fages, Sgt. José Francisco Ortega, and Fathers Juan Crespí and Francisco Gómez, on August 2, 1769. They camped at the present site of Bassett on the San Gabriel River and reached a spot occupied by the ancient Indian village of Yang-na, what is now Downey Avenue, near North Broadway. (Los Angeles Public Library Photo Collection.)

Within the church grounds, cloister archways and the quadrangle are pictured around 1921. The friars stroll under the arbors on a peaceful day. (Los Angeles Public Library Photo Collection.)

An afternoon's impression of Los Angeles Plaza, and La Placita, in 1920 offers a leisurely gathering place on a sunny day for its many residents. (Los Angeles Public Library Photo Collection.)

Surviving centuries, historical items at the church include vestments, sacred altarpieces, artworks, candlesticks, and many pieces reminding visitors of the lives once lived within the church, which serves the Spanish heritage in the city today. (Los Angeles Public Library Photo Collection.)

Pictured in 1925, an intricate altar at La Placita was set to honor an occasion of Our Lady the Queen of the Angels of the Porciúncula. Feast days are in August. (Los Angeles Public Library Photo Collection.)

At La Placita in 1981, John Romani, the field test coordinator of archeology, explores the earliest building and remaining foundations as well as clues to the culture and lifestyle of the first settlers. (Los Angeles Public Library Photo Collection.)

La Placita is pictured in 1899, prior to the espadaña reconstruction.

The quadrangle view frames the old arbor and shrine at La Placita in a photograph taken in 1937. In 1833, mission Indians congregated to retrieve mission properties in San Diego, San Juan Capistrano, San Gabriel, and San Bernardino. Thwarted by soldiers, the Indian attacks at the Santa Catalina Mission in Baja and the San Bernardino Asistencia totally destroyed them. In 1842, many Quechans, Kamias, Cahuillas, and Hamakhavas became more aggressive, attempting to recover surrounding ranchos. At the same time, an increasing tide of fur trappers, traders, and immigrants was moving west. (Los Angeles Public Library Photo Collection.)

San Bernardino Asistencia was established in 1819 as a sub-mission of Mission San Fernando Rey de España. The original asistencia functioned as an outpost to provide grazing for mission cattle. Today's buildings are reproductions constructed in the 1930s. (Los Angeles Public Library Photo Collection.)

Rebuilt in 1960, San Bernardino Asistencia was dedicated as a California Historical Landmark known to the general public as "the Asistencia." Today, the facility operates as a branch of the San Bernardino County Museum. (Los Angeles Public Library Photo Collection.)

In 1925, the County of San Bernardino acquired the mission property; all remaining historic materials were salvaged, and construction of a new, six-room structure commenced in 1926. The restoration was completed in 1937 with a freestanding campanario, even though none had existed previously. The original mission site was approximately one mile east of the original estancia site. (Los Angeles Public Library Photo Collection.)

San Bernardino Asistencia was abandoned in the 1830s, and remaining mission buildings were used by José del Carmen Lugo as part of his rancho grant. After sale to the Mormons, it was occupied by Bishop Nathan C. Tenney in the 1850s and by Dr. Benjamin Barton in the 1860s. (Los Angeles Public Library Photo Collection.)

The Rancho Camulos estancia is part of the large original Rancho San Francisco and lies on the trail extending between Mission San Buenaventura and Mission San Fernando Rey de España. The Camulos adobe house is probably the best preserved and most typical of all of California's older rancho houses once visited by early Spanish friars.

Behind the small chapel at Rancho Camulos, an original fountain stands centered near the adobe house. The home hosted many guests on the path established between missions along El Camino Real. A granary building was erected in 1804 and soon another, each over 100 feet long and made from adobe brick.

This church is near Tejón Pass in the mountains outside Los Angeles. Pedro Fages, an early acting governor of Alta California, rode north across the Canyon of the Grapes from San Diego to San Luis Obispo in 1772 in pursuit of Spanish army deserters in rugged mountainous territory.

This native home is on Rancho El Tejón, which covers nearly 270,000 acres. The historic Tejon Ranch is the largest contiguous expanse of private land in California. It was owned by US general Edward F. Beale in the 1850s, and he employed natives of the area as vaqueros and farmers. Thousands of Native Americans performing ancient rituals at the mouth of Tejón Creek were described by Bishop William Ingraham Kip on a visit in 1855.

In 1852, Gen. E.F. Beale, appointed the first superintendent of Indian affairs, had by 1854 successfully concentrated over 1,000 natives on Téjon Indian Reservation while developing his adobe residence, pictured around 1888. The 1st Dragoons of the US Army were stationed to keep watch and completed constructing Fort Téjon between 1854 and 1861.

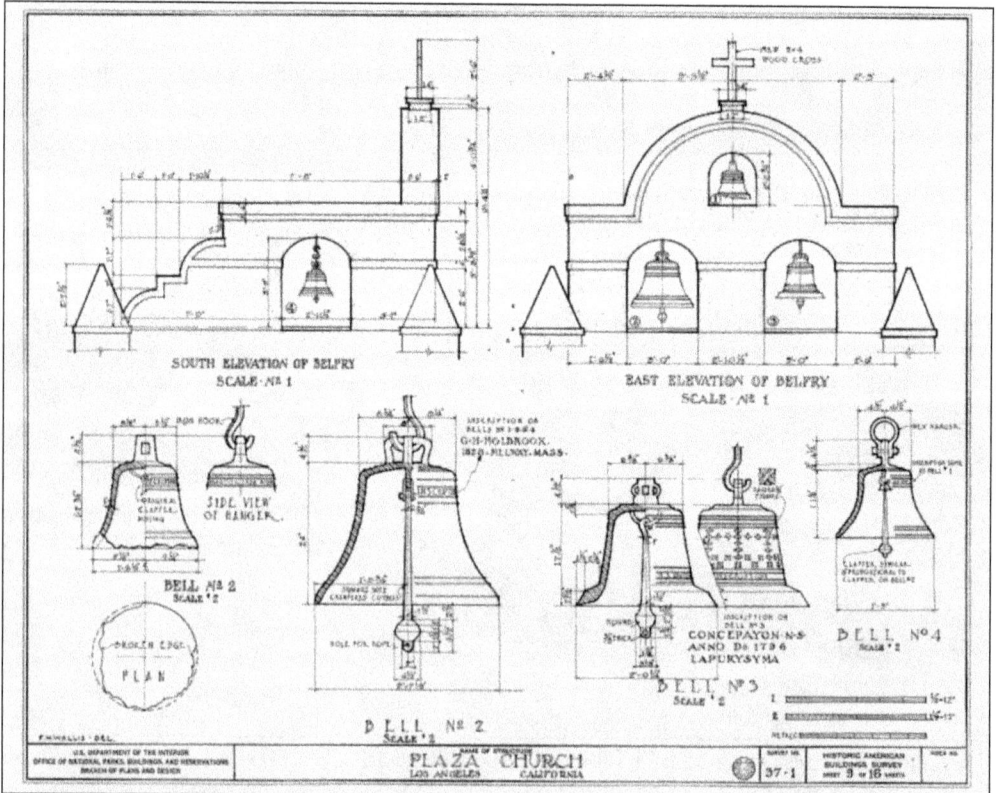

The espadaña bell wall replaced an older wooden gazebo. The church's brick front was installed in 1861 and completed in 1882, replacing deteriorating adobe bricks according to remarks from the 1936 Historic American Buildings Survey.

Five

MISSIONS PAST AND PRESENT
TOURING EL CAMINO REAL

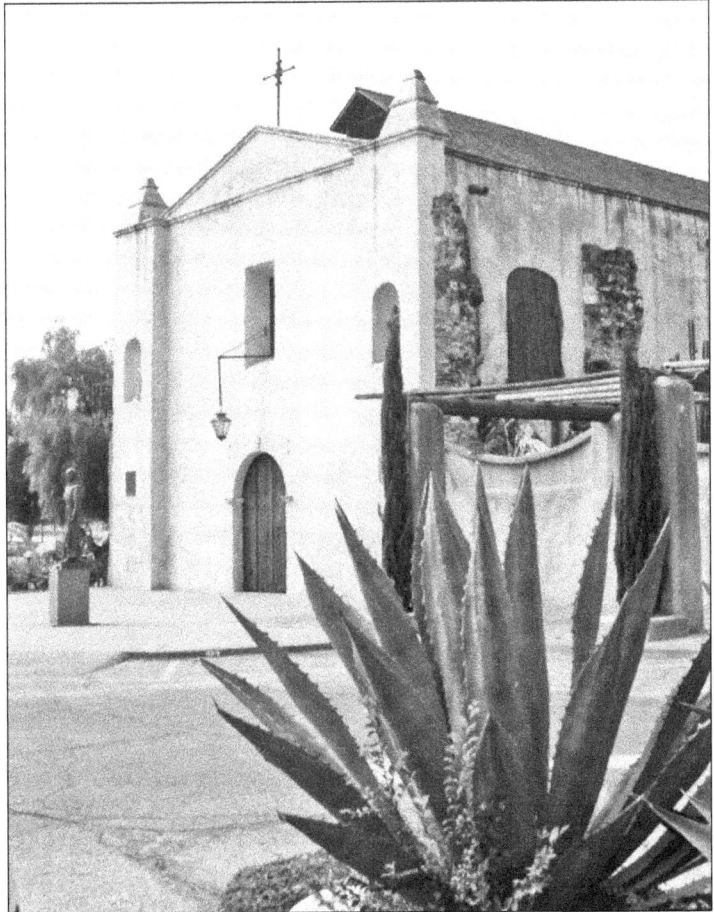

The Mission San Gabriel, Arcángel, is open to visitors, and the grounds have been clearly marked with important historical artifacts and signage. It is the fourth of California's Spanish missions and features architectural influences of Spanish-Moorish design more than other missions with its striking profile. (Author's collection.)

Pyramidal finials atop each supportive buttress create the most elegant profile of all Spanish California missions. The design of Mission San Gabriel, Arcángel, is unlike any other in California. The mission was completed in 1805 and, after the 1812 earthquake, was rebuilt by 1828. (Author's collection.)

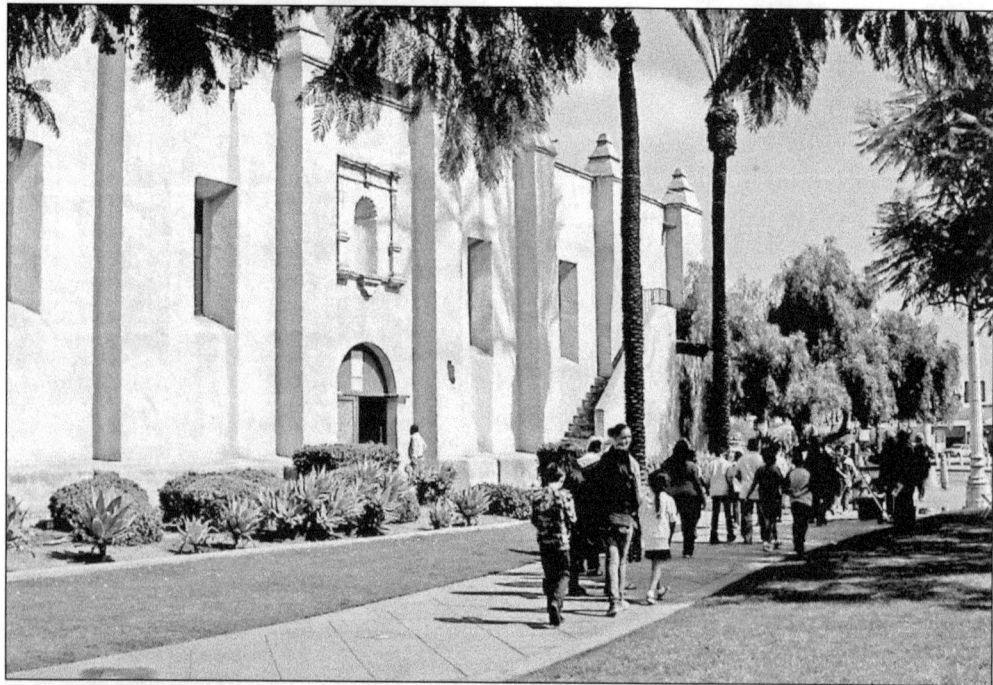

Children in fourth-grade classes choose a mission project to study to absorb the historic Spanish impact in California, and these students are studying Mission San Gabriel, Arcángel. The relationship of the native inhabitants, missionaries, and soldiers from the earliest founding was steeped in complexity. (Author's collection.)

The dissimilar sized bells of the bell wall is a unique feature among all early California missions. The first bell tower had fallen during the 1812 earthquake, and a new espadaña was built at the rear of today's mission. The relationship with the Tongva natives was not always harmonious, and skirmishes were often a part of the earliest period at Mission San Gabriel. In time, it became a very productive mission. (Author's collection.)

Capt. Juan Bautista de Anza reached California from the Sonoran Desert by way of the Colorado River and Mojave Desert on his first trip in 1774, accompanied by Padre Francisco Garces. De Anza stayed to recuperate at San Gabriel and eventually settled San Francisco in 1776 after his second arduous 1,000-mile desert journey. (Author's collection.)

The Mission San Gabriel features an original hand-hammered cooper font resting on a large granite block in the baptistery, with an ornately recessed cove for artwork and a decorated dome. It was the fourth California mission and was founded by Fathers Pedro Benito Cambón and Angel Somera in 1771. Mission San Gabriel, Arcángel, is at 428 South Mission Drive in San Gabriel and can be reached at 626-457-3035 or www.sangabrielmissionchurch.org. (Author's collection.)

Founded by Fr. Junípero Serra in 1776, Mission San Juan Capistrano was the seventh in Alta California. The expansive grounds still contain the ruins of the Great Stone Church, a relic of the most elaborate church undertaken by the Franciscan friars. (Author's collection.)

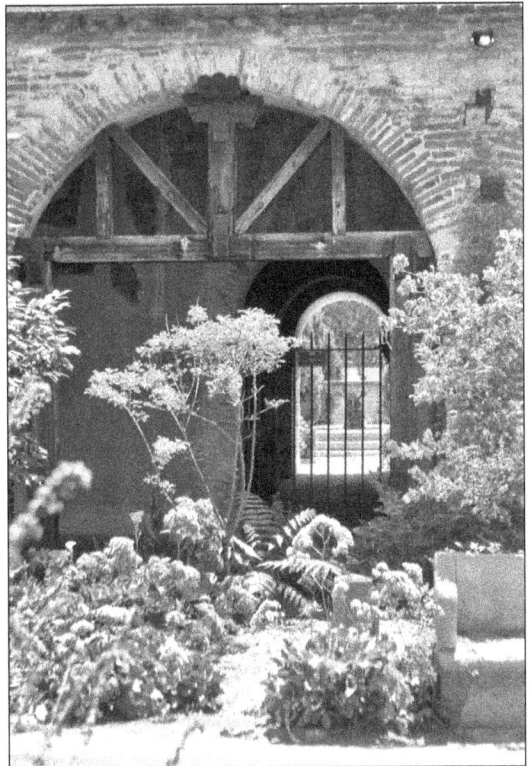

Mission San Juan Capistrano was a self-sustaining mission until 1839. By 1845, it was sold by the Mexican governor, and was reclaimed by the Church in 1865 after a written proclamation presented by Pres. Abraham Lincoln, now in an archive held on the mission grounds. (Author's collection.)

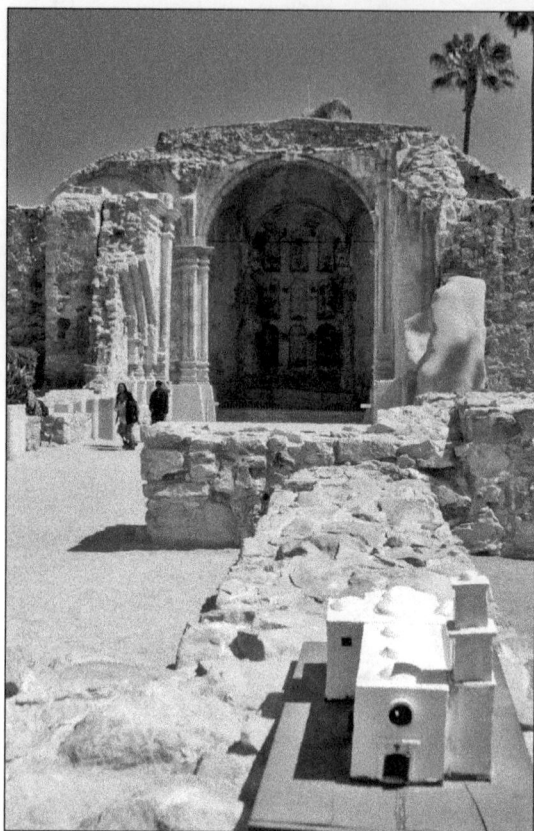

In the 1860s, efforts were organized to restore the Great Stone Church at Mission San Juan Capistrano using dynamite to remove two of the remaining dangerous stone roof domes. Gaps in the stone walls were repaired with adobe bricks. The efforts were abandoned after a severe storm destroyed new shingle roofing and most of the repair work. (Author's collection.)

The courtyard within the mission's large quadrangle was set in pervasively quiet surroundings. Juaneño mission Indians had been promised transfer of lands after the Mexican secular laws affected Mission San Juan Capistrano's settlements. However, this agreement ended, favoring the Californios who settled many surrounding ranchos. (Author's collection.)

The beautiful gilded reredos was installed with the renovations of 1922. It was stored in Los Angeles after being shipped from Barcelona, Spain, in 1903. The piece was installed within the Serra Chapel at Mission San Juan Capistrano to add an authentic historical character to the only surviving chapel where Father Serra had held services. (Author's collection.)

The seventh California mission was founded by Fr. Junípero Serra in 1776. Mission San Juan Capistrano is at 26801 Ortega Highway in San Juan Capistrano and can be reached at 714-234-1300 or www.missionsjc.com. (Author's collection.)

Old El Camino Real is the largest surviving adobe of the Spanish mission period, and today welcomes visitors to explore the mission's museum inside. (Author's collection.)

The Cordoba-styled fountain was constructed in the 1800s and is original to the mission grounds but was moved about 300 feet closer to the mission gardens in the 1920s. The fountain design emulates a rosette of a Moorish star pattern with the massive fountainhead at the center. (Author's collection.)

The Mission San Fernando Rey de España church was rebuilt from the foundations according to original measurements, finally solving the weakened deterioration of its adobe walls, especially following the 1976 Sylmar earthquake damages.

An original mission fountain stands along the side of El Camino Real in front of the mission's "Long Building," or convento. It fed water to the mission quadrangle in the original days. The park was designed and installed by developer L.C. Brands in the 1920s. (Author's collection.)

Mission San Fernando Rey de España's beautiful interior was rebuilt and rededicated in 1974. Rebuilt to exact measurements, the mission's courtyard leads to the side entry of the church and the cemetery. On the mission grounds are the last memorial and resting place of Hollywood star Bob Hope and his wife, Dolores. (Author's collection.)

The "Long Building" convento facade faces Old El Camino Real and measures 243 by 50 feet. The two-story adobe building has withstood the elements and remains the oldest, largest adobe building standing. It welcomes visitors to the mission museum with early art, photographs, milling machines, and artifacts used by mission Indians and the first friars.

The 17th mission, founded by Fr. Fermín Francisco de Lasuén in 1797, was named for Saint Ferdinand III, King of Spain. Mission San Fernando Rey de España and the Historical Museum & Archival Center, North Los Angeles County, are at 15151 San Fernando Mission Boulevard in Mission Hills and can be reached at 818-361-0186. (Author's collection.)

21. San Francisco de Solano

★ SACRAMENTO

20. San Rafael Arcángel

SAN FRANCISCO

6. San Francisco de Asis "Dolores"

8. Santa Clara de Asis

14. San José de Guadalupe

15. San Juan Bautista

12. Santa Cruz

MONTEREY   2. San Carlos Borroméo de Carmelo

13. Nuestra Señora de la Soledad

3. San Antonio de Padua

16. San Miguel Arcángel

5. San Luis Obispo de Tolosa

11. La Purísima Concepción

19. Santa Inés

10. Santa Barbara

SANTA BARBARA   9. San Buenaventura

17. San Fernando Rey de España

4. San Gabriel Arcángel

LOS ANGELES   7. San Juan Capistrano

18. San Luis Rey de Francia

1. San Diego de Alcalá

SAN DIEGO

PACIFIC OCEAN

El Camino Real, or "the Royal Way," begins in San Diego. Along the 650-mile trail, California's first Franciscan missionaries, accompanying tenacious explorers, founded 21 Spanish missions. The landmarks of the first landfall in San Diego in 1769 include the first Spanish mission, presidio, and mission colony, founded by Fr. Junípero Serra with Gaspar de Portolá, explorer and governor of Baja California. Control by Franciscan missionaries and the Spanish Crown lasted 54 years. By 1850, California became the 31st state of the Union.

BIBLIOGRAPHY

Berger, John A. *The Franciscan Missions of California*. Garden City, NY: Doubleday & Co., 1948.

Chapman, Charles E. *A History of California: The Spanish Period*. New York: The Macmillan Co., 1921.

Elder, Paul. *The Old Spanish Missions of California*. San Francisco: Paul Elder and Co., 1913.

Forbes, Jack G. *Native Americans of California and Nevada*. Happy Camp, CA: Naturegraph Publishers, 1982.

Gudde, Erwin G. *1,000 Place Names*. Berkeley and Los Angeles: UC Press, 1965.

Hoover, Mildred Brooke, Hero Eugene Rench, and Ethel Grace. *Historic Spots in California*. Stanford: Stanford University Press, 1953.

Kimbro, Edna E. and Julia G. Costello with Tevvy Ball. *The Missions of California*. Los Angeles: J. Paul Getty Museum, 2009.

Morgado, Martin J. *Junípero Serra: A Pictorial Biography*. Monterey: Siempre Adelante Publishing, 1991.

Mornin, Edward and Lorna. *Saints of California*. Los Angeles: J. Paul Getty Museum, 2009.

Sunset Editors. *The California Missions: A Pictorial History*. Menlo Park: Sunset Publishing Corp., 1991.

Wright, Ralph B. *California's Missions*. Los Angeles: Sterling Press, 1950.

Visit us at
arcadiapublishing.com

www.ingramcontent.com/pod-product-compliance
Lightning Source LLC
Chambersburg PA
CBHW050659110426
42813CB00007B/2044